5 appears at top right.

6

We're walk-ing in the air,_____ we're danc-ing in the mid - night

sky,_____ and eve-ry-one who sees us greets us as we fly._____

Also available from Faber Music:

The complete piano score of *The Snowman*: H0002

Highbridge Music

ADMINISTERED BY
Faber Music Ltd., 3 Queen Square, London WC1

ISBN 0-571-58001-7

9 780571 580019